D1018996

I HAVE ABANDONED
MY SEARCH FOR TRUTH,
and am now looking
for a good fantasy©

More Brilliant Thoughts®
by
Ashleigh Brilliant

creator of *Pot-Shots*® and author of

I MAY NOT BE TOTALLY PERFECT,
BUT PARTS OF ME ARE EXCELLENT©

Published by
Woodbridge Press Publishing Company
Santa Barbara, California 93111

1997 Printing

Published by
Woodbridge Press Publishing Company
Post Office Box 209
Santa Barbara, California 93102

Copyright © 1980, by Ashleigh Brilliant

All rights reserved

World rights reserved. This book or any part thereof may not be reproduced in any form whatsoever without the prior written permission of Woodbridge Press Publishing Company, except in the case of brief passages embodied in critical reviews or articles. Brilliant Thoughts® ("Pot-Shots")℗ are each separately copyrighted Up to but no more than five may be reproduced or quoted in any one critical review or article, provided that correct copyright acknowledgement is also included. Inquiries concerning all other uses of Brilliant Thoughts® ("Pot-Shots")℗ should be directed to Ashleigh Brilliant, 117 West Valerio Street, Santa Barbara, California 93101

Distributed simultaneously in the United States and Canada

Printed in the United States of America.

Library of Congress Cataloging-in-Publication Data

Brilliant, Ashleigh, 1933-
   I have abandoned my search for truth, and am
now looking for a good fantasy

1. Epigrams. 2. American wit and humor, pictorial. I. Title.

PN 6281.B67   818'.5402   80-22852
ISBN 0-912800-89-5
ISBN 0-912800-90-9 (pbk.)

POT SHOTS and BRILLIANT THOUGHTS are Registered Trade Marks.

10

This Book . . .

Acknowledgements and Dedication

The following people have all been partly responsible for what you see here. They deserve much of the credit, and nearly all of the blame. They certainly deserve the dedication:

My father and mother, Victor and Amelia Brilliant. I am the product of their own dedication.

My uncle, Marsh Adler, of Los Angeles, who imported me into the United States in 1955, and has ever since wondered why.

Dorothy Low Tucker Brilliant, since 1968 my devoted consort and reluctant co-conspirator.

My sister, Myrna Brilliant, who has kindly permitted her 1944 image to appear on POT-SHOT No. 241.

Marjorie Low and Dorothea Tucker of Santa Barbara, who have always helped me hide, even when nobody was looking for me.

Allen Carrico, a better friend than most people are ever lucky enough to have.

Netter Worthington, quondam Dean of the Seven Seas Division of Chapman College, who enabled me to fulfill my wildest fantasy, of teaching college while sailing around the world (1965-67).

John Henderson, hard-bitten newspaperman, who nevertheless somehow became the world's first publisher of POT-SHOTS (San Francisco, 1967).

Doug Kaplan of San Francisco, my friend since our childhood in Washington, D.C., and for many years my most faithful POT-SHOTS distributor.

Elliot Steinberg of Aviva, Inc., who first recognized the wide market potential of my work and my name.

Bob Reed of the Chicago Tribune-New York News Syndicate, to whom, since 1975, millions of newspaper readers have owed their daily POT-SHOT.

Don Fraser of St. Helena, California, who is the nearest thing my gospel has to an evangelist.

Tom McCarthy and Ron Laurie of Townsend & Townsend, my copyright and trademark lawyers, who have done such good work in my behalf, and have been so very well paid for it.

Howard Weeks, the visionary publisher of this book, and of its predecessor, I MAY NOT BE TOTALLY PERFECT, BUT PARTS OF ME ARE EXCELLENT.

The people at the following licensed companies, who, by publishing my works on their various products, have shown that great thoughts need not be confined to books, monuments, and rest-room walls:

Freelance, Inc., Willow Grove, Pennsylvania.
Dodo Designs, Tunbridge Wells, Kent, England.
Monogram of California, San Francisco.
Perma-Greetings, Inc., Maryland Heights, Missouri.
Artex Manufacturing Co., Overland Park, Kansas.
Argus Communications (DLM, Inc.), Niles, Illinois.

And also Jerry Wolf, Jon and Margo Showstack, Marilyn Arnett Lewis, Stan and Virginia Sargent, Sol Morrison, Nat Hersh, Dr. Jerry Marmorstein, E.W. Maynard Potts, Hartley and Margie Kern, the Irwin Wunderman Family, Myra Currin, Larry Kirsch, Roger and Nancy Sharp, Ben Jones, Jan Menschel, Gerry Goldstein, Bill Espenshade, Jimmee Stein.

Albert Field, Barbara Kramer, Mike Gross, Don Signorovitch, Obafemi Odeyemi, Herb Caen, Beverley Jackson, Chet Holcombe, Kim and Bill Downey

—all of whom have, in one way or another, provided me with inordinate amounts of aid and comfort as I stumbled through the years towards bringing you whatever it is I now bring you.

And of course, special mention must be made of all those people, equally or even more deserving, who are not listed here, but who, by their friendship, patronage, and encouragement, and/or their opposition, neglect, and desertion, have helped to shape the shaper of this opus.

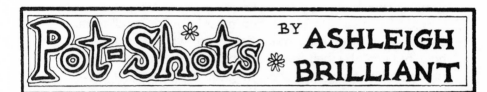

© BRILLIANT ENTERPRISES 1975

POT-SHOTS NO. 826.

I HAVE ABANDONED
MY SEARCH FOR TRUTH,

AND AM
NOW LOOKING

FOR A GOOD
FANTASY.

Ashleigh Brilliant

Introduction

Who Goes Here?

At last your eyes are meeting my words! Or perhaps we have met in this way before. In either case, welcome to my mind. If this is, by happy chance, a first visit, allow me to introduce myself: My name is Ashleigh Brilliant, and I am (to a certain very limited extent) at your service.

I was born on December 9, 1933, and have lived mainly in England (mostly London) and America (mostly California). My background is lower-middle class, Anglo-Jewish, cosmopolitan, and academic. In 1964 I somehow acquired the degree of Ph.D. in History at the University of California at Berkeley. Since then, I have had three different careers — first as a gifted but unsettled, and perhaps unsettling, college teacher; next as a sort of mock-hippie-guru in San Francisco; and most recently as a semi-respectable businessperson, author, "syndicated cartoonist," and husband in Santa Barbara.

My object is to help all of us to deal with reality, by presenting it in palatable, digestible morsels. The works assembled in this book began their public life in 1967 as a series of separate

11

postcards, published, as they still are, by my own company, under the collective name of POT-SHOTS.® They come to me at various times (rarely, I'm glad to say, in the middle of the night), often prompted by something somebody has said, but usually as a simple attempt to express and satirize my own thoughts and feelings. I write down the idea immediately; then, if not satisfied with what I have written (and my standards are maddeningly high), I work on it until I am, or until I abandon it in despair. This whole process can take years.

I follow numerous very strictly self-imposed rules of composition, the two most important being that no POT-SHOT may exceed seventeen words, and that the words and expressions used must be understood as easily as possible, by the widest possible range of people, with no impediment (such as rhyme, puns, or idioms) to translation into other languages. After the writing, I do the art-work (which is often the most difficult part of all), trying very hard to make it fit the words without dominating them.

Knowing the Book, and Throwing the Book

To increase your possible enjoyment of this deliberately different form of literature, I suggest that you feel no compulsion to absorb the whole book at once. Most people find that they can't stay very long in my head without beginning to feel faint — even though I myself have to stay here all the time. Also, you may enjoy reading some of my lines aloud to other people in a group. (They were written partly with this purpose in mind.) Another thing you can do, should do, *must* do, is send for my catalogue of postcards (see last page). This will help you to avoid the possible temptation to cut the book up in order to send different pieces to different people.

This is my second book of this kind in less than two years. I had thought that the public might be satisfied with one, at least for some considerable time; but my publisher apparently feels we have struck pay-dirt, and that there's no harm in sinking more shafts.

If you have read I MAY NOT BE TOTALLY PERFECT, BUT PARTS OF ME ARE EXCELLENT (published in 1979), you may recall that one of the hazards of my profession as a coiner of epigrams is

12

their susceptibility to theft — forcing me to take very vigorous action to defend my copyright. Some people have even questioned whether literary works as short as mine are actually entitled to copyright protection at all, especially if only the words are copied, and not the art. In order to get a clear ruling on this, I took a particularly flagrant case to Federal District Court, which may be of some interest to you, since it involved, among other things, the title of this book (a POT-SHOT first copyrighted in 1975).

The case has already attracted considerable attention, and, as it becomes more widely known, I hope it may have the effect of encouraging other serious writers to explore the field of very short literary forms. It is officially known as: Ashleigh Brilliant v. W.B. Productions, Inc. (U.S. District Court, Los Angeles, Civil Action No. CV 79-1893-WMB; judgment entered October 22, 1979.) At issue were the words of three of my POT-SHOTS which the defendants had been selling in the form of T-shirt transfers, without any credit or authorization, and despite repeated requests and warnings for them to stop. (The first being the title of this book, the other two lines were: I MAY NOT BE TOTALLY PERFECT, BUT PARTS OF ME ARE EXCELLENT and I'M IN SEARCH OF MYSELF — HAVE YOU SEEN ME ANYWHERE?) Judge William Matthew Byrne, hitherto best-known for his role in the Pentagon Papers trial, heard the case. He found that my copyrights were "valid, subsisting, and enforceable," and awarded me damages, fees, and costs totalling $18,000. The case was not appealed, and the judgment has been paid in full. As you may imagine, this was a very satisfying result, and makes one suspect that, even in this world, there may indeed be a certain amount of justice.

The Name of Me

While the names of my books are property I have had to fight to retain, my own name is something I have sometimes wished I could lose. Actually, Ashleigh Brilliant is not my real name. My real name is Ashleigh Ellwood Brilliant. I have never much minded the "Brilliant" part, because I was apparently born with an I.Q. to go with it; but, as a child, I hated the "Ashleigh Ellwood." For some obscure and sensitive family

I KNOW
WHAT'S WHAT
AND WHO'S WHO,

BUT I HAVE
NO IDEA
WHY'S WHY.

© BRILLIANT ENTERPRISES 1977.

Ashleigh Brilliant

14

reason, I was never called by either of these names, except in anger. Instead, throughout my childhood, although my father's name was Victor, I was called "Junior" (except at Hebrew School in Washington D.C., 1941-46, where I had the Hebrew name of Avrahom).

Fortunately, at the schools I attended in England during my adolescence, only first initials and not first names were used for boys, so there, instead of "Junior Brilliant," I signed myself as "J. Brilliant." When I had to explain what the "J." stood for, it became embarrassing to say "Junior," and for a few years I went under the name of John Brilliant, although that was a name I didn't like either.

As my twenty-first birthday approached, in 1954, I became obsessed with the notion that the question of my name was a problem which I must now settle once and for all. Either I must accept my real name (which I had kept a close secret, and which still seemed most unpleasant), or I must choose a totally new one, and stick with it. While struggling with this terrifying choice, I happened one day to see a poster in the student lounge of University College, London, which I was attending at the time. It proclaimed in big letters the forthcoming appearance of a speaker I had never heard of before, whose name was ASH BROWN. Teetering as I then was on my personal brink, this name greatly impressed me. "Here is a man," I said to myself, "who has a name something like mine, and who is not afraid to declare it thus to the world. Surely then, I can have the courage to do likewise." Then and there I made the Great Decision, and next day I put up the following notice on a college bulletin-board:

THE PERSON HITHERTO KNOWN AS JOHN BRILLIANT
WISHES IT TO BE KNOWN THAT HIS REAL NAME IS
ASHLEIGH ELLWOOD BRILLIANT, AND IN FUTURE
HE WISHES TO BE KNOWN AS SUCH.

Thus the die was cast, and I felt great relief, and a certain exaltation. But, when I came back the following day to look proudly again at my notice, I found that some diabolical wit had put quotation marks around the word "SUCH."

An even greater shock was in store for me when I happened to look again, more closely, at the ASH BROWN poster. For the first

A SMALL ADVANCE EVERY DAY

WILL EVENTUALLY TOTAL

MUCH LESS THAN A BIG ADVANCE EVERY DAY.

Ashleigh Brilliant

POT SHOTS No.1699.©1980 Ashleigh Brilliant

16

time, I saw some small dots which somehow I hadn't noticed before. The name was not "Ash" at all — those were just his initials: A.S.H. Brown!

But it was too late by then to re-think my position. All my friends were already calling me Ashleigh (fortunately, "Such" Brilliant never caught on); and, after a bit of getting used to, it wasn't really so bad. Of course, little did I then dream that one day, after I had developed a medium of expression actually brilliant enough to go with it, I would find the name Ashleigh Brilliant one of my greatest social and economic assets.

Self-Made Self

Everybody thinks, and some of us even occasionally utter, crazy things, often combining truth with absurdity. My particular gift has been to be able to isolate such thoughts, and express them in a terse, witty form. And my particular success (such as it is) has come about through having the audacity to market these trifles as if they were a valuable form of merchandise. I have even been able to hire many of them out to respectable companies, who print them, along with my magical name, on various manufactured products, such as T-shirts, tote-bags, and cocktail napkins. My written permission is grandly called a "license"; and the rental fee is even more grandly called a "royalty," though there's certainly nothing royal about it these days, and even kings never went so far as to charge for their own words. There is today, I have gradually discovered, a whole "licensing industry" revolving around such bizarre transactions. Grown men and women compete savagely for the "rights" to associate their particular product with some imaginary character, some film title, some celebrity's image. But, as far as I know, I am the first and still the only person in the world to make a career out of licensing his own "Brilliant thoughts."

Do You Read Me?

The business called "syndication," in which I have been involved since 1973, is a special form of licensing, enabling me to be a daily guest in a host of newspapers. Since there had never been anything like POT-SHOTS, nothing like it had ever been syndicated before, and this is obvious from the mail it has provoked. For one thing, readers have not known whether to think of it as a "cartoon" or as a "column." Some emotionally delicate persons have clearly regarded it as a private daily message somehow inserted into their newspaper for their eyes alone. One unfortunate woman sent me a detailed personal reply to every POT-SHOT every day for years. At first this thrilled me, but I came to have doubts when, for no apparent reason, she started calling me "Bob," and began to say that she had seen me flying over her house in my helicopter. I tried to deter her by breaking my silence to write and ask her to at least send me some money to help keep my helicopter going; but she just ignored this, and kept on writing. It was not until the news-paper in her town ran a feature article about me, with a photo-graph, that her letters suddenly and permanently stopped. It's bad enough to have to believe that your most faithful fan is insane; but even worse, somehow, to find that one look at your face can break whatever spell you had over her.

I hasten to add that even apparently normal people also write to me, often saying how much personal meaning they have found in a particular POT-SHOT, or in many, most, or even all of them. Statistically, of course, the odds are on my side. If I fire broadly enough, often enough, in the general direction of enough people, there's always a good chance of scoring plenty of hits. (Hence, at least in part, the name "POT-SHOTS," which also derives from the idea of filling my cooking-pot, since this strange activity is, after all, my chief means of livelihood.) Some-times I can only speculate as to what particular nerve I may have hit. The following, for example, is the entire unedited text of one unsigned "fan-letter":

> Dear Sirs:
>   Several months ago you rang an article in Pot
> Shots. It read WHY IS THE HUSBAND OR THE WIFE
> ALWAYS THE LAST TO KNOW? Please run this again.
>   Thanks.

Almost the only adverse mail I receive tends to be of a religious nature, but is usually more compassionate than criti-cal. A few devout souls feel sorry for me when I say things like

"IF YOU SEE GOD, TELL HIM I'M LOOKING FOR HIM." They send me tracts and Bibles, and urge me to mend my ways. Sometimes I try to soften their wrath by pointing out that I do also have messages which say things like "SCIENCE MAY SOMEDAY DISCOVER WHAT FAITH HAS ALWAYS KNOWN." And I take personal comfort in the fact that clergymen of many different persuasions have always formed a large and prominent group among the many thousands of mail-order customers for my postcards. But of course, like any other good scriptural text, the POT-SHOTS litany, freely interpreted as the situation may require, can supply truths to support or oppose almost any conceivable moral or intellectual position (and many inconceivable ones). Indeed, that may be precisely why I am now at last so publicly willing to call off my own search for truth and so ready to join all the rest of humanity in the search for any good available fantasy.

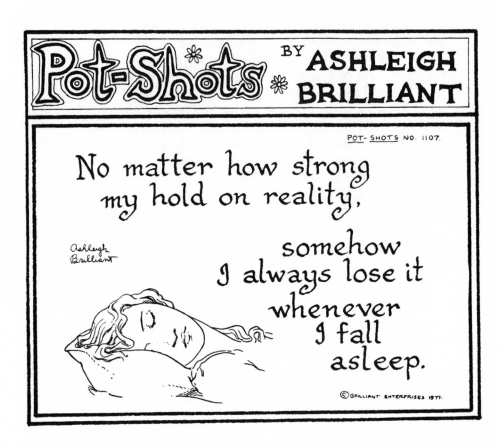

Pot-Shots BY ASHLEIGH BRILLIANT

POT-SHOTS NO. 1107.

No matter how strong
my hold on reality,

somehow
I always lose it
whenever
I fall
asleep.

© BRILLIANT ENTERPRISES 1977.

The Body—A Strange Place To Live

One thing we all have in common is the at least nominal command of a body of some kind. It keeps us constantly busy supplying its various needs, yet insists on changing in ways over which we still have very little control, and ultimately, one way or another, completely discontinues itself, leaving us totally in the lurch. We know it is a thing of marvelous ingenuity — apparently the best vehicle yet developed for traveling forward through periods of time on Earth ranging up to about a hundred years. Yet it has strange quirks and vulnerabilities, and can be totally incapacitated by a microscopic germ or a paralyzing emotion. It can be trained to a certain extent, but has its own peculiar ways of doing things, which we simply have to accept. Its methods of feeding, eliminating, and reproducing are almost too grotesque to be believed. About a third of its total time is spent in a strange resting-state called "sleep."

Most of these odd characteristics are apparently traceable to earlier times and conditions which our bodies have not yet learned no longer prevail. The learning which does take place occurs in a dense, unlikely, and rather unlovely organ called the brain. Somehow it seems there is more of us in our brain than there is anywhere else. In some mysterious way, thinking is the same as being.

I make no apologies, therefore, for actually thinking in public, right before your very eyes. It's really my only excuse for being here at all.

© BRILLIANT ENTERPRISES 1977.

LIFE IS
AN INCURABLE CONDITION:

Ashleigh Brilliant

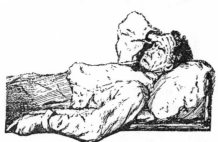

THE ONLY
KNOWN TREATMENT
IS TO TRY
TO KEEP
THE PATIENT
COMFORTABLE.

THE LAST TIME I FELT GOOD WAS AT 10:00 A.M.

ABOUT NINE YEARS AGO.

Ashleigh Brilliant

POT SHOTS No.1663.©1980 Ashleigh Brilliant

I'M NOT YET SURE WHAT I'LL DIE OF,

BUT HOPE IT'S NOT SOMETHING I COULD HAVE PREVENTED.

POT SHOTS No.1743.©1980 Ashleigh Brilliant

POT-SHOTS NO. 196

REPORTS OF MY BEING ALIVE AND WELL HAVE BEEN GROSSLY EXAGGERATED.

Ashleigh Brilliant

© BRILLIANT ENTERPRISES 1970

POT-SHOTS NO. 1348.

I HIDE THINGS
FROM YOU
THAT I WOULDN'T
DREAM OF HIDING
FROM ANYBODY ELSE.

Ashleigh Brilliant

© BRILLIANT ENTERPRISES 1977.

© BRILLIANT ENTERPRISES 1976

POT-SHOTS NO. 958.

HOW CAN I PROVE

I'M NOT CRAZY

TO PEOPLE WHO ARE?

Ashleigh Brilliant

POT-SHOTS NO. 201 ©BRILLIANT ENTERPRISES 1976 Ashleigh Brilliant

YOU REACHED ME JUST IN TIME

I WAS BEGINNING TO FEEL CONFIDENT AGAIN.

NOTHING ELSE CAN DISTURB ME

WHEN YOU'RE DISTURBING ME.

Ashleigh Brilliant

POT SHOTS No.1660 ©1980 Ashleigh Brilliant

©BRILLIANT ENTERPRISES 1976. POT-SHOTS NO. 994.

NOT NOW

AND MAYBE NOT LATER EITHER.

Ashleigh Brilliant

© ASHLEIGH BRILLIANT 1973

POT-SHOTS NO 1476

EVERY TIME I DO IT **AT LEAST PROVES THAT**

I CAN STILL DO IT.

Ashleigh Brilliant

© BRILLIANT ENTERPRISES 1968

POT-SHOTS NO. 67

I'M VERY GOOD AT EATING —

CAN YOU TELL ME WHERE THEY NEED EATERS?

Ashleigh Brilliant

POT-SHOTS NO. 833

Ashleigh Brilliant

THE SECRET OF GOOD COOKING

IS TO ASSOCIATE WITH A GOOD COOK.

© BRILLIANT ENTERPRISES 1975.

26

© BRILLIANT ENTERPRISES 1976

HOW CAN I EAT ANY FOOD?

IT ALL

COMES FROM

LIVING THINGS!

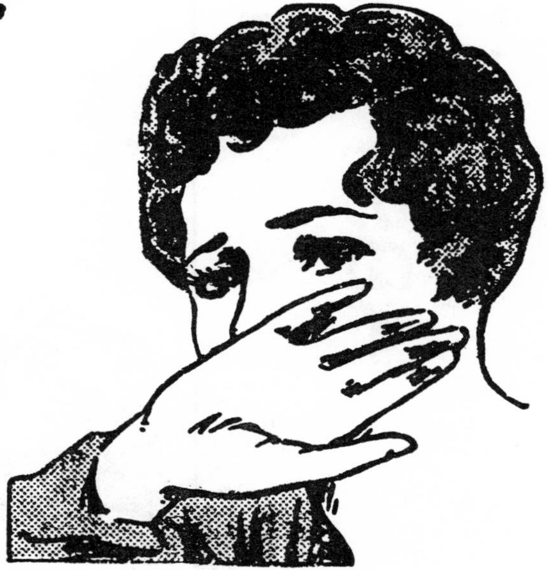

Ashleigh Brilliant

27

©BRILLIANT ENTERPRISES 1977.

Ashleigh Brilliant

I TRIED ABSTINENCE ONCE,

BUT I DIDN'T LIKE IT.

©BRILLIANT ENTERPRISES 1977.

SOMEHOW I REACHED EXCESS WITHOUT EVER NOTICING WHEN I WAS PASSING THROUGH SATISFACTION.

Ashleigh Brilliant

IF CHOCOLATE COULD TEACH, I WOULD BY NOW BE EXTREMELY WELL-EDUCATED.

POT SHOTS No.1648.©1980 Ashleigh Brilliant

Ashleigh Brilliant

© BRILLIANT ENTERPRISES 1974.

POT-SHOTS NO. 622

AFTER BREAKFAST, DOES ANYTHING MATTER

BUT LUNCH?

Ashleigh Brilliant

Pot-Shots

Ashleigh
Brilliant

YOU MAY HAVE A PLACE IN MY LIFE,

BUT
I HAVEN'T TIME
TO HELP YOU
FIND IT.

POT SHOTS No.1655.©1980 Ashleigh Brilliant

We Two, and Me Too

Sooner or later, we become aware of the existence of other bodies in the world besides our own. This is generally a welcome discovery, though in some ways difficult to become accustomed to. Eventually, we find that we are part of a whole category of things, loosely called "people." With other members of this rather exclusive group, through a process called "communication," we learn to exchange information, ideas, and feelings, which sometimes also lead to the exchange of insults and blows.

Two people communicating, we find, are always more than twice as many as one person alone. For they consist invariably of two "you's" and two "me's." This enormously complicates the human predicament, but also offers certain consolations. If there must be conflict, misunderstanding, and apathy, two people can bear them more easily than one solitary self. And besides, with any luck at all, there is always the possibility of mutual assistance, friendship, and even love.

But, no matter how close the relationship may become, any other person is always something of a mystery and something of a risk, and there will always be certain ambivalences of feeling, as I try to show in many of the following messages. After all, "I" was always here first in my life, before "you" ever came along.

POT SHOTS NO. 261 ©BRILLIANT ENTERPRISES 1971

IT'S YOUR OWN FAULT
FOR NOT LIVING UP TO
MY IMPOSSIBLY HIGH STANDARDS

Ashleigh Brilliant

**WE'LL
ALWAYS
STAY
ON
GOOD
TERMS,**

Ashleigh Brilliant

**SO LONG
AS THEY'RE
MY TERMS.**

POT SHOTS No 1731 ©1980 Ashleigh Brilliant

Ashleigh Brilliant

Well,
if you don't like
my opinion
of you,

you can always

improve.

POT SHOTS No.1702 ©1980 Ashleigh Brilliant

© BRILLIANT ENTERPRISES 1972

FOLLOW ME

IT'S BETTER FOR US
TO BE LOST TOGETHER.

Ashleigh
Brilliant

**ONE GOOD REASON
FOR TRUSTING ME
IS THAT
MANY OTHER
FOOLISH PEOPLE
ALREADY
TRUST ME.**

Ashleigh
Brilliant

POT SHOTS No 1895 ©1980 Ashleigh Brilliant

**EVERY NOW AND THEN,
I DO
THE RIGHT
THING,**

**JUST TO
CONFUSE
YOU.**

Ashleigh
Brilliant

© ASHLEIGH BRILLIANT 1975

33

©BRILLIANT ENTERPRISES 1977 POT-SHOTS NO. 1255.

Ashleigh
Brilliant

YOU AND I ARE BOTH EXACTLY ALIKE,

BUT THERE THE RESEMBLANCE ENDS.

©BRILLIANT ENTERPRISES 1976. POT-SHOTS NO. 938

IF ONLY THE RIDICULOUS THINGS THAT ARE IMPORTANT TO ME

COULD BE AS IMPORTANT TO YOU.

Ashleigh Brilliant

LOOK OUT!

YOU'RE STEPPING ON MY VALUES!

POT SHOTS No.1676.©1980 Ashleigh Brilliant

I WANT YOU, HAPPINESS, AND CHOCOLATE,

BUT NOT NECESSARILY IN THAT ORDER.

POT SHOTS No.1722.©1980 Ashleigh Brilliant

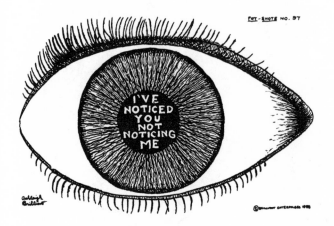

I'VE NOTICED YOU NOT NOTICING ME

POT-SHOTS NO. 1028.

WHAT GOOD ARE YOU IF YOU DON'T NEED ME?

© BRILLIANT ENTERPRISES 1977

© BRILLIANT ENTERPRISES 1973. POT-SHOTS NO. 850.

HOLD ON TO ME:

SOMEDAY I MAY BE QUITE VALUABLE.

HAVE I RUINED YOUR LIFE,

Ashleigh Brilliant

OR WAS IT RUINED ALREADY?

© BRILLIANT ENTERPRISES 1977

Ashleigh Brilliant

WHAT'S THE GOOD OF BEING FORGIVEN, IF I HAVE TO PROMISE NOT TO DO IT AGAIN?

© BRILLIANT ENTERPRISES 1977.

COME OVER TO MY SIDE OF THE ARGUMENT: THE VIEW IS ALWAYS SO CLEAR FROM HERE.

© BRILLIANT ENTERPRISES 1977.

Ashleigh Brilliant

© ASHLEIGH BRILLIANT 1979.

WHY AREN'T YOU MORE GRATEFUL WHEN I PROVE HOW WRONG YOU'VE BEEN?

Ashleigh Brilliant

IT'S NOT FAIR
THE WAY
YOU KEEP
RETALIATING

Ashleigh Brilliant

© BRILLIANT ENTERPRISES 1970.

AGAINST MY
UNPROVOKED ATTACKS.

© BRILLIANT ENTERPRISES 1970   POT-SHOTS NO. 203

I KNOW
YOU'RE STRONGER
THAN I AM...

BUT IT'S
YOUR TURN
TO SURRENDER.

Ashleigh Brilliant

Ashleigh Brilliant

I GAVE YOU
EVERYTHING,

AND ALL
YOU EVER GAVE ME
WAS
YOURSELF.

POT SHOTS No 1710 ©1980 Ashleigh Brilliant

By accepting you
as you are,
I do not
necessarily
abandon
all hope
of your
improving.

POT SHOTS No.1687.©1980 Ashleigh Brilliant

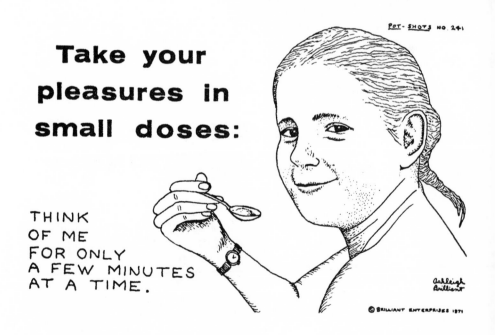

**Take your
pleasures in
small doses:**

THINK
OF ME
FOR ONLY
A FEW MINUTES
AT A TIME.

© BRILLIANT ENTERPRISES 1971

ARE WE HAVING A RELATIONSHIP --

Or just doing research on each other?

© BRILLIANT ENTERPRISES 1974.

© BRILLIANT ENTERPRISES 1974

WONDERFUL!
You have some of my favorite problems.

© BRILLIANT ENTERPRISES 1977.

POT-SHOTS NO. 1277.

Ashleigh Brilliant

YOU ARE ONLY PART OF MY PROBLEM ~

ANOTHER PART IS ME.

Ashleigh Brilliant

AS SOON AS I DECIDE WHAT TO DO ABOUT ME,

I'LL CONSIDER WHAT TO DO ABOUT YOU.

POT SHOTS No.1693.©1980 Ashleigh Brilliant

POT- SHOTS NO. 748.

Ashleigh
Brilliant

PLEASE LET ME KNOW

IF THERE'S ANY FURTHER TROUBLE

I CAN

GIVE YOU.

© BRILLIANT ENTERPRISES 1975.

I'D LOVE TO ASSIST YOU
OUT OF
YOUR DIFFICULTIES,

INTO
MINE.

POT SHOTS No.1742.©1980 Ashleigh Brilliant

POT-SHOTS NO. 1336.

WE'VE BEEN THROUGH SO MUCH TOGETHER,

AND
MOST OF IT
WAS YOUR FAULT.

© BRILLIANT ENTERPRISES 1377.

Ashleigh
Brilliant

POT-SHOTS NO. 1192.

DON'T BE AFRAID— I'M RIGHT BEHIND YOU

USING YOU
AS A SHIELD.

Ashleigh
Brilliant

© BRILLIANT ENTERPRISES 1977.

SOMETIMES
I NEED
WHAT
ONLY YOU
CAN
PROVIDE:

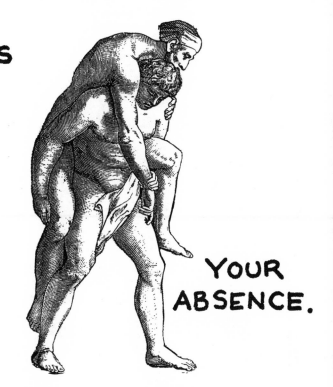

YOUR
ABSENCE.

Ashleigh Brilliant

POT SHOTS No.1661.©1980 Ashleigh Brilliant

©BRILLIANT ENTERPRISES 1975 *Ashleigh Brilliant*   POT-SHOTS NO. 763

MY CLEVEREST TRICK

WILL BE

TO BECOME OLDER...

AND OLDER,

AND EVENTUALLY

DISAPPEAR COMPLETELY.

Pot-Shots BY ASHLEIGH BRILLIANT

© BRILLIANT ENTERPRISES 1974.

POT-SHOTS NO 584

Fortunately
in my work
there's always
a choice:

I can choose
to do it willingly
or
unwillingly.

Ashleigh Brilliant

How the World Works

In case you haven't noticed it, the world is a very busy place. Various groups of people are constantly engaged in working with, for, and against each other, as if their lives depended on it (which they sometimes do). Willy-nilly, we find ourselves caught up in jobs, companies, industries, economic systems — striving, competing, maneuvering, with not much time (in many cases) for thinking about what we are doing, and what is being done to us.

The work-game has many strange rules. One is that you're not supposed to enjoy it (or else it isn't work). Another is that you must somehow, in some way, be involved in producing something that somebody else wants. This leaves nobody except those who are not playing the game to produce all those very important things that nobody wants. Among such items are one of my own principal products: unpopular thoughts.

The thought-market is in fact even more unpredictable than the stock market. The public is a peculiar animal. Without ever giving any clear explanation, it will consume certain of my thoughts with relish, while turning up its nose at others which in my view are equally fine, pure, and delicious. This becomes very apparent when the thoughts are marketed as individual cards. In a recent popularity survey of 1,000 different POT-SHOTS, only one message was not chosen by a single person out of hundreds of people surveyed. Of course, it turned out to be one of my own personal favorites. Who can account for such things? The message (since I know you are curious) is POT-SHOT No. 693, which says, "ONE POSSIBLE REASON WHY I DON'T BELIEVE IN FATE IS THAT I WASN'T FATED TO."

© BRILLIANT ENTERPRISES 1975

POT-SHOTS NO. 858

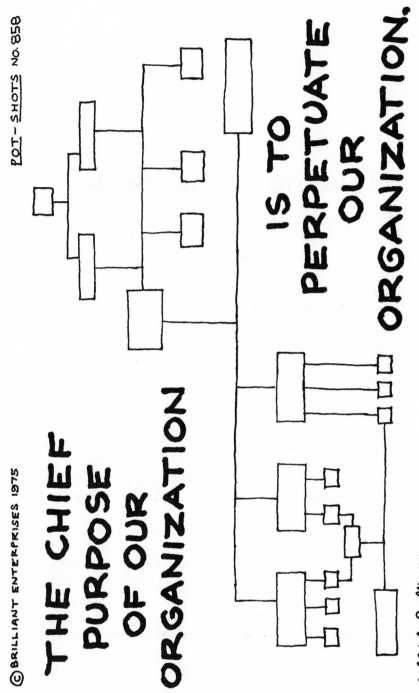

THE CHIEF
PURPOSE
OF OUR
ORGANIZATION
IS TO
PERPETUATE
OUR
ORGANIZATION.

Ashleigh Brilliant

48

Ashleigh
Brilliant

BEING
IN DEBT

IS

ONE WAY
OF PROVING
THAT
IT'S POSSIBLE
TO HAVE
LESS THAN NOTHING.

© BRILLIANT ENTERPRISES 1977.

Ashleigh
Brilliant

POT-SHOTS NO. 1248

© BRILLIANT ENTERPRISES 1977.

OUR MEETINGS ARE HELD
TO DISCUSS MANY PROBLEMS
WHICH WOULD NEVER ARISE
IF WE HELD FEWER MEETINGS.

THE GREAT WORK MUST GO FORWARD

Ashleigh Brilliant

AS SOON AS WE ALL FIND SOMEBODY ELSE TO DO IT.

© BRILLIANT ENTERPRISES 1977.

ANYBODY WHO TRIES TO GET BETWEEN ME AND MY WORK

Ashleigh Brilliant

HAS A GOOD CHANCE OF SUCCEEDING.

© BRILLIANT ENTERPRISES 1977.

©BRILLIANT ENTERPRISES 1976.

Ashleigh
Brilliant

To function
effectively
here,
you need
to have
the proper
Lack of Spirit.

©BRILLIANT ENTERPRISES 1969

I'M NOT GETTING PAID MUCH
FOR STAYING ALIVE

BUT IT'S GOOD EXPERIENCE

Ashleigh
Brilliant

©ASHLEIGH BRILLIANT 1973.

Ashleigh
Brilliant

An unfair method
sometimes used
to gain control of
an organization
is: to attend all the meetings.

© BRILLIANT ENTERPRISES 1968

Ashleigh
Brilliant

USE YOUR OWN JUDGMENT

THEN DO AS I SAY

© BRILLIANT ENTERPRISES 1971

PLEASE SURRENDER NOW

BEFORE I HAVE TO
OFFER YOU
BETTER TERMS.

Ashleigh
Brilliant

POT-<u>SHOTS</u> NO. 990.

Ashleigh
Brilliant

IT'S MY IDEA!

I STOLE IT FIRST!

© BRILLIANT ENTERPRISES 1976.

© BRILLIANT ENTERPRISES 1977.

POT-<u>SHOTS</u> NO. 1323.

Ashleigh
Brilliant

DON'T BE NERVOUS —

JUST REMEMBER:

ALL MISTAKES WILL BE SEVERELY PUNISHED.

IF MY WORK SATISFIES ME, HOW COULD IT POSSIBLY NOT SATISFY YOU?

Ashleigh Brilliant

POT SHOTS No.1705. ©1980 Ashleigh Brilliant

© BRILLIANT ENTERPRISES 1969

BEFORE BURNING
THESE PAPERS,

LET ME
MAKE SURE
THEY'RE IN

ALPHABETICAL ORDER.

Ashleigh Brilliant

Pot-Shots BY ASHLEIGH BRILLIANT

© BRILLIANT ENTERPRISES 1975.

POT-SHOTS NO. 793.

LIFE HAS BEEN VERY CONFUSING, BECAUSE I'VE BEEN DIFFERENT AGES AT DIFFERENT TIMES

Is It Time?

Nobody knows what time *is*, but everybody knows what time *does*. Among other things (and always, of course, in correct chronological order), time builds and levels mountains, heals wounds, eliminates the unfit, and dries up spilled milk. Despite being so busy, however, time usually takes its time, and always seems to have time for playing games with us — making good times fly and bad times drag, causing newspapers to become out of date before we have finished reading them, and turning the milk we didn't spill sour.

But, although rather mysterious in many ways, time does attempt to communicate with us, through a medium known since Biblical times as "The Writing On The Wall." And here time and I have something in common. I have always thought of myself as a sort of super-graffitist, with the whole world to write on. And at least one authority on the subject, Robert Reisner, author of *Graffiti: 2000 Years of Wall Writing,* has seen the connection, kindly claiming to see in my POT-SHOTS "much of the quality of the best graffiti: wry humor, surrealist quality, and underlying truth."

Time is traditionally depicted as an old man carrying a scythe, presumably to cut down everything in his path. But my own favorite image (perhaps just as fanciful, but at least not so grim) is that of an eternal strip of cinematic film, possibly a loop, the "show" playing endlessly, one frame at a time, giving us the "illusion" of things changing, moving, and happening.

Whatever your own view, I'm glad that we were at least able to spend this much of our time together.

ALL MY LIFE, I'VE BEEN CHANGING ~

WHEN WILL I FINALLY BECOME WHAT I'M REALLY SUPPOSED TO BE?

©BRILLIANT ENTERPRISES 1977. Ashleigh Brilliant

©BRILLIANT ENTERPRISES 1976.

POT-SHOTS NO 939.

Ashleigh Brilliant

I still have many of my old dreams,

but some of the colors have faded.

EVERYTHING THAT SHOULD STAY THE SAME IS CHANGING,

AND EVERYTHING THAT SHOULD CHANGE IS STAYING THE SAME.

Ashleigh Brilliant

©BRILLIANT ENTERPRISES 1977.

POT-SHOTS NO. 1076

MY TIME

IS WORTH MUCH MORE THAN ANYBODY COULD POSSIBLY AFFORD TO PAY FOR IT.

© BRILLIANT ENTERPRISES 1977

Ashleigh Brilliant

POT-SHOTS NO. 955.

Ashleigh Brilliant

I NEED MORE WAYS TO SAVE TIME,

AND MORE THINGS TO DO WITH THE TIME I SAVE.

© BRILLIANT ENTERPRISES 1976

© BRILLIANT ENTERPRISES 1971

JUST WHEN I WAS GETTING USED TO YESTERDAY...

Ashleigh Brilliant

ALONG CAME TODAY.

© BRILLIANT ENTERPRISES 1975.

Ashleigh Brilliant

I'M EXPECTING A MAJOR CHANGE IN MY LIFE SOMETIME WITHIN THE NEXT 30 YEARS.

SOONER OR LATER, I'LL BE PUNCTUAL.

© BRILLIANT ENTERPRISES 1972

© BRILLIANT ENTERPRISES 1974.

THE BEST THING ABOUT BEING TOO LATE

IS THAT THERE'S NO MORE NEED TO HURRY.

Ashleigh
Brilliant

©ASHLEIGH BRILLIANT 1978.

INSIDE EVERY
OLDER PERSON,

THERE'S A
YOUNGER
PERSON,

WONDERING
WHAT HAPPENED.

62

TIME FLIES!

POT-SHOTS NO. 1108.

I'M ALREADY AS OLD
AS MY PARENTS WERE
WHEN THEY WERE MY AGE.

© BRILLIANT ENTERPRISES 1977.

Ashleigh Brilliant

© BRILLIANT ENTERPRISES 1970

THERE'S NOTHING WRONG
WITH GROWING OLDER,
    BUT WHERE DOES IT LEAD?

Ashleigh Brilliant

POT-SHOTS NO. 150

POT-SHOTS NO. 358

CHINESE: 人生如寄

NO WONDER
I FEEL SO TIRED —
I'M OLDER NOW
THAN I'VE
EVER BEEN BEFORE.

Ashleigh Brilliant

© BRILLIANT ENTERPRISES 1972

© BRILLIANT ENTERPRISES 1975.

NOBODY WANTS OLD PEOPLE
WHO ARE ALWAYS SAYING
THAT NOBODY WANTS OLD PEOPLE.

Ashleigh Brilliant

© BRILLIANT ENTERPRISES 1977

DEAD?

I DIDN'T EVEN KNOW HE WAS STILL ALIVE.

Ashleigh Brilliant

I'VE ALWAYS WANTED TO GO BACK IN TIME ~

I HAVE RELATIVES THERE.

POT SHOTS No.1732.©1980 Ashleigh Brilliant

Ashleigh Brilliant

WHEN YOU BECOME DEAD, YOU JOIN A VERY LARGE ORGANIZATION.

POT SHOTS No.1754.©1980 Ashleigh Brilliant

Ashleigh Brilliant

IF I MUST GO INTO ETERNITY,

I'D PREFER TO GO BY THE SCENIC ROUTE.

POT SHOTS No.1736.©1980 Ashleigh Brilliant

Ashleigh Brilliant

©BRILLIANT ENTERPRISES 1975

POT-SHOTS NO. 726.

EVENTUALLY, I HOPE I'LL LEARN TO FACE DEATH

—IF I LIVE LONG ENOUGH.

Ashleigh Brilliant

© ASHLEIGH BRILLIANT 1979

IF I DIE
BEFORE DOING
EVERYTHING
ON MY LIST,

TO WHOM
SHOULD I
LEAVE THE LIST?

Ashleigh Brilliant

Ashleigh Brilliant

IT'S HARD
TO FACE
TOMORROW,

BUT
IT'S EASIER
THAN FACING
NO TOMORROW.

POT SHOTS No. 1728. ©1980 Ashleigh Brilliant

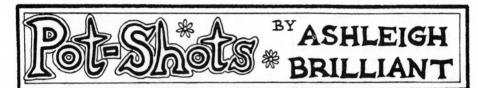

Pot-Shots BY ASHLEIGH BRILLIANT

©BRILLIANT ENTERPRISES 1974

POT-SHOTS NO. 459

DO YOUR BEST
TO SATISFY ME —

Ashleigh
Brilliant

— THAT'S ALL
I ASK
OF EVERYBODY.

Only Human

Human-ness is what makes us all have more in common with each other than we have with anything else. Being human is a great (even if involuntary) responsibility, and necessarily involves great risk. It always comes at a time when you are not ready for it, and all of your training must be on-the-job.

From inside our human heads, we see a world of stunning complexity. The only reason why we are not completely overwhelmed is that we are not required to deal with all of it at once. We try to make whatever sense of it we can, deriving a surprising variety of interpretations from exactly the same evidence. In my own case, I feel more comfortable dealing, more or less at random, with single small aspects of reality, rather than trying to scan the whole picture in one sweep. By publishing my thoughts separately, I have been able to avoid responsibility for any relationship between them. I do have great admiration for the skill of a good novelist in creating a single unified structure out of many thousands of words; but within the narrow confines of a single POT-SHOT, I at least try to say something which seems true and different and worth saying. Readers may sometimes disagree with what they think I mean. But then, misunderstanding and being misunderstood is only another inevitable part of being human.

ALL I WANT
IS TO BE TREATED
LIKE EVERYONE ELSE,

Ashleigh Brilliant

NO MATTER HOW
REVOLTINGLY DIFFERENT
I AM.

© BRILLIANT ENTERPRISES 1977.

Ashleigh Brilliant

I WANT
TO ESCAPE FROM
ALL THE BAD THINGS,
AND TAKE
ALL THE GOOD THINGS
WITH ME.

© BRILLIANT ENTERPRISES 1977.

JOY TODAY
IS NOT ENOUGH—

I WANT
FULLY GUARANTEED
FUTURE JOY.

Ashleigh Brilliant

© BRILLIANT ENTERPRISES 1977.

© ASHLEIGH BRILLIANT 1978.

SOMETIMES, A PLEASANT SURPRISE WOULD BE EVEN MORE PLEASANT IF IT WEREN'T SO MUCH OF A SURPRISE.

I'VE GOT NOTHING ELSE TO DO, SO I MIGHT AS WELL HURRY.

POT SHOTS No 1695 ©1980 Ashleigh Brilliant

Ashleigh Brilliant

I SEE SOME PLEASURE COMING! — EVERYBODY GET IN LINE BEHIND ME.

POT SHOTS No. 1715 ©1980 Ashleigh Brilliant

© BRILLIANT ENTERPRISES 1974.

WHY WASTE TIME
GETTING ORGANIZED,
WHEN THERE ARE
SO MANY
MORE IMPORTANT THINGS
I COULD BE DOING?

Ashleigh Brilliant

DON'T RUSH ME ~
I'LL FACE TODAY
TOMORROW.

Ashleigh Brilliant

POT SHOTS No. 1751 *1980 Ashleigh Brilliant

© BRILLIANT ENTERPRISES 1969

HAVE YOU
HAD ANY
GOOD MOODS
LATELY?

Ashleigh Brilliant

SUCCESSFUL PEOPLE ARE OFTEN VERY BORING TO OTHERS WHO ARE NOT SUCCESSFUL,

AND TO OTHERS WHO ARE.

POT SHOTS No.1740.©1980 Ashleigh Brilliant

Ashleigh Brilliant

POT-SHOTS NO. 1405.

THE BEST THING ABOUT FAILING IS THAT IT MAKES NOBODY JEALOUS.

Ashleigh Brilliant

©ASHLEIGH BRILLIANT 1979.

Ashleigh
Brilliant

SOME PEOPLE CAN FIND
ALL THE
PEACE OF MIND THEY NEED
IN A GOOD,
SATISFYING,
CONFLICT.

© ASHLEIGH BRILLIANT 1975.

74

© BRILLIANT ENTERPRISES 1973

BE KIND TO UNKIND PEOPLE :
THEY PROBABLY NEED IT MOST.

Ashleigh Brilliant

LET'S PUT THE BLAME WHERE IT BELONGS:

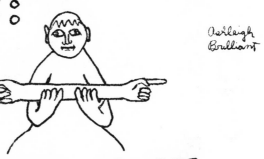

Ashleigh Brilliant

ON SOMEBODY ELSE.

© BRILLIANT ENTERPRISES 1977.

IF ONLY OUR GREAT THINKERS COULD LEARN TO TALK, AND OUR GREAT TALKERS COULD LEARN TO THINK!

© BRILLIANT ENTERPRISES 1977

POT-SHOTS NO. 12GG.

Ashleigh Brilliant

76

©BRILLIANT ENTERPRISES 1974.

I ALWAYS KNOW
THE RIGHT THING TO SAY,

after the
right time to say it
has passed.

©BRILLIANT ENTERPRISES 1974

IT ALWAYS HELPS PROVE
HOW RIGHT YOU ARE

IF YOU
WAVE YOUR ARMS
AND JUMP
AND SCREAM.

©BRILLIANT ENTERPRISES 1974

THE MORE SURE YOU ARE,

THE MORE WRONG
YOU CAN BE.

Ashleigh
Brilliant

© BRILLIANT ENTERPRISES 1974.

I'M PERFECTLY
WILLING TO BE
JUDGED AND
CRITICIZED,

BUT ONLY BY
GOD AND HISTORY.

78

PLEASE SPARE ME THE GHASTLY DETAILS OF YOUR HAPPINESS.

POT SHOTS No.1753.©1980 Ashleigh Brilliant

IF YOU MAKE ONE OR TWO RIDICULOUS ASSUMPTIONS,

YOU'LL FIND EVERYTHING I SAY OR DO TOTALLY JUSTIFIED.

Ashleigh Brilliant

POT SHOTS No.1671.©1980 Ashleigh Brilliant

© BRILLIANT ENTERPRISES 1975.

AS SOON AS I CAN FIND A GOOD POSITION,

I INTEND TO TAKE A FIRM STAND.

ashleigh Brilliant

ashleigh Brilliant

YOU KNOW I'LL ALWAYS BE FAITHFUL

TO THE CURRENT TREND.

© BRILLIANT ENTERPRISES 1977.

POT-SHOTS NO. 65   © BRILLIANT ENTERPRISES 1968

PLEASE DON'T
SPOIL EVERYTHING

BY TELLING ME THE TRUTH

© BRILLIANT ENTERPRISES 1975.

POT-SHOTS NO. 857.
Ashleigh Brilliant

*I have never
behaved
improperly,*

BUT I
RESERVE THE RIGHT
TO DECIDE
WHAT IS PROPER.

Lonely Human

Loneliness is no crime, and no disgrace. Some of my best friends are occasionally lonely, and I myself am rumored to have experienced the condition. But it can unfortunately be contagious, which is why lonely people tend to be avoided, thus of course making them all the more lonely.

It may be that our inherent sense of loneliness as individuals is only a reflection of the inevitable cosmic loneliness which besets our species, still (as of this writing) the only one known of its kind in the entire universe. But modern society also plays its part, confronting us with so many people, situations, choices, and commands all at once that defensively we fall back upon the only being who is really always there — the good old self.

Much of my "fan-mail" comes from people who tell me that my POT-SHOTS help them to feel less alone. Apparently, what cheers a lonely person more than almost anything else is to hear some other lonely soul lamenting, especially if the lamentation is pungently packaged in seventeen words or less.

© BRILLIANT ENTERPRISES 1977.

I CAN NO LONGER FACE LIFE,

SO I'VE DECIDED
TO GO THROUGH
THE REST OF IT
BACKWARDS.

Ashleigh
Brilliant

Ashleigh
Brilliant

I probably
deserve the
medal for
loneliness...

FOR DISTINGUISHED LONELINESS

but who
would think of
nominating me?

© BRILLIANT ENTERPRISES 1970

WHY AM I ALWAYS SO ALONE IN MY STRUGGLE TO HAVE MY OWN WAY?

POT SHOTS No.1683. ©1980 Ashleigh Brilliant

POT-SHOTS NO. 1170.

I ALWAYS CONSIDER IT A GOOD DAY WHEN NOBODY MURDERS ME.

© BRILLIANT ENTERPRISES 1977.

Ashleigh Brilliant

I PREFER
TO BE DISCOVERED
LITTLE BY LITTLE,

RATHER
THAN
BEING

TOTALLY EXPOSED
ALL AT ONCE.

© ASHLEIGH BRILLIANT 1979.

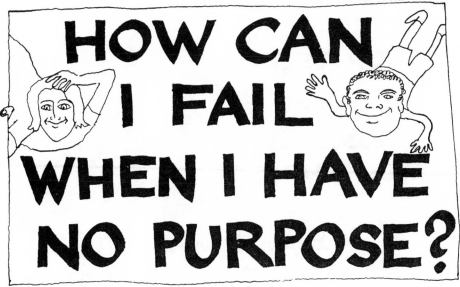

HOW CAN I FAIL WHEN I HAVE NO PURPOSE?

© BRILLIANT ENTERPRISES 1977

Ashleigh Brilliant

© ASHLEIGH BRILLIANT 1979

DESPITE MY DETERMINATION,
I KEEP RUNNING INTO

A SERIOUS
OBSTACLE,
CALLED
"OTHER PEOPLE."

Ashleigh Brilliant

87

IT TOOK
COURAGE
TO DO
SOME OF
THE THINGS

Ashleigh Brilliant

WHICH I NOW WISH
I'D NEVER DONE.

© ASHLEIGH BRILLIANT 1978.

© ASHLEIGH BRILLIANT 1979

MY BIGGEST PROBLEM
IS WHAT TO DO
ABOUT ALL
THE THINGS
I CAN'T DO
ANYTHING ABOUT.

Ashleigh Brilliant

SOMETIMES THE BEST WAY TO BE USEFUL IS TO GET OUT OF SOMEBODY'S WAY.

Ashleigh Brilliant

© ASHLEIGH BRILLIANT 1979

YES, BUT I'M A VERY WELL-ORGANIZED FAILURE.

Ashleigh Brilliant

© BRILLIANT ENTERPRISES 1977.

EVERYTHING
I AM TODAY
I OWE
TO PEOPLE
WHOM
IT IS NOW
TOO LATE
TO PUNISH.

POT SHOTS No.1747.©1980 Ashleigh Brilliant

© BRILLIANT ENTERPRISES 1976   POT-SHOTS NO. 902.

YOU'RE MISSING SO MUCH

BY NOT
HAVING

ALL THE
TROUBLES
I HAVE.

POT-SHOTS NO. 1459.

MANY PEOPLE
HAVE SPENT
THEIR WHOLE LIVES

WORRYING ABOUT

THE SAME THINGS
I'M SPENDING MINE

WORRYING
ABOUT.

© ASHLEIGH BRILLIANT 1978.

© BRILLIANT ENTERPRISES 1977

BEWARE!

I CAN DO
GREAT HARM
TO MYSELF,
AND BLAME IT
ON YOU.

Ashleigh Brilliant

MY WAY
MAY NOT BE
RIGHT FOR YOU

OR EVEN
FOR ME.

POT SHOTS No 1745 ©1980 Ashleigh Brilliant

Ashleigh Brilliant

NO MATTER
WHAT YOU
MAY THINK,
I DO NOT
ENJOY SUFFERING.

AT LEAST,
NOT VERY MUCH.

POT SHOTS No 1866 ©1980 Ashleigh Brilliant

THINGS ARE GRADUALLY FALLING INTO PLACE

ON TOP OF ME.

Ashleigh Brilliant

© BRILLIANT ENTERPRISES 1977.

POT-SHOTS NO 1521.

AT ANY MOMENT,
I COULD
SUDDENLY
START BEING
A BETTER
PERSON ~

BUT WHICH
MOMENT
SHOULD I
CHOOSE?

© ASHLEIGH BRILLIANT 1979

POT-SHOTS NO. 1075

I WANT
TO BE
MORE
THAN
I AM,

Ashleigh
Brilliant

BEFORE
I BECOME
LESS.

© BRILLIANT ENTERPRISES 1977.

© BRILLIANT ENTERPRISES 1577.

POT-SHOTS NO. 1221.

Ashleigh
Brilliant

IT'S HARD
TO REMAIN TRUE
TO A CHANGING SELF.

THE MOST GLORIOUS THING ABOUT MY STRUGGLE

IS THAT IT CAN NEVER POSSIBLY BRING ME ANY GLORY.

Ashleigh Brilliant

POT SHOTS No.1658.©1980 Ashleigh Brilliant

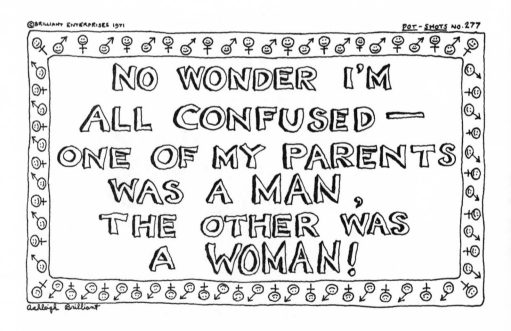

©BRILLIANT ENTERPRISES 1971   POT-SHOTS NO.277

NO WONDER I'M ALL CONFUSED — ONE OF MY PARENTS WAS A MAN, THE OTHER WAS A WOMAN!

Ashleigh Brilliant

© BRILLIANT ENTERPRISES 1977.

JUSTICE WILL TRIUMPH IN THE END —

THAT'S WHY I'M SO WORRIED.

Ashleigh Brilliant

Pot-Shots BY ASHLEIGH BRILLIANT

POT-SHOTS NO. 1297.

WHEN I FIND
TRUE WISDOM,
I'LL LET YOU KNOW,

(IF LETTING
YOU KNOW
STILL SEEMS
IMPORTANT.)

Ashleigh Brilliant

© BRILLIANT ENTERPRISES 1977.

All In the Mind (I Think)

One of the hardest times to think is while trying to operate something as complicated as a human body in a place as fraught with dangers and difficulties as planet Earth. But that seems to be the only time most of us have, and the uncertainties of the situation indeed give us plenty to think about. Under such names as "Religion," "Philosophy," "Science," and "Morality," various explanations have been offered of how we come to be here and what we ought to do about it. Each has its myths and dogmas, its prophets and holy texts. So I see no reason for withholding my own set of scriptures, not handed to me on any mountain-top, but gathered with considerable effort from the many nooks and crannies of my own mind. As you will notice, each one is individually numbered (the numbers indicating roughly the order in which they were first published), and some of my more devoted followers, to save time (and perhaps to express reverence) refer to them, when communicating with each other, by citing the number rather than by quoting the words. Innocent bystanders are occasionally amused and baffled at the spectacle of two or more POT-SHOTS addicts gleefully calling numbers back and forth — a game unfortunately too mentally demanding for yours truly, the cult founder.

IT WOULD BE EASIER FOR ME TO REJECT ALL ESTABLISHED VALUES,

Ashleigh Brilliant

IF I KNEW WHAT THEY WERE.

POT-SHOTS No. 1721. © 1980 Ashleigh Brilliant.

© Brilliant Enterprises 1976.

POT SHOTS No. 997.

Ashleigh Brilliant

THINGS CAN ONLY GET BETTER,

OR WORSE,

OR STAY THE SAME,

OR NOT BE WHAT WE SUPPOSED.

© BRILLIANT ENTERPRISES 1970

IF YOU
SEE GOD,

TELL HIM
I'M LOOKING
FOR HIM.

I WANT ETERNAL LIFE,
OR SOMETHING JUST AS GOOD.

© ASHLEIGH BRILLIANT 1979

I CAN DO ANYTHING
GOD WANTS
ME TO DO,

BUT THE INSTRUCTIONS
MUST BE
VERY CLEAR.

Ashleigh
Brilliant

©ASHLEIGH BRILLIANT 1975.

THERE
REALLY IS
A GOD,

BUT THE
GOVERNMENT
IS HUSHING
IT UP.

Ashleigh
Brilliant

©BRILLIANT ENTERPRISES 1975.

THE UNIVERSE
IS
AN ISLAND,

SURROUNDED BY
WHATEVER IT IS
THAT
SURROUNDS UNIVERSES.

©BRILLIANT ENTERPRISES 1977.

IF EVERYTHING
IS PART OF A WHOLE,

WHAT IS
THE WHOLE
PART OF?

©BRILLIANT ENTERPRISES 1977.

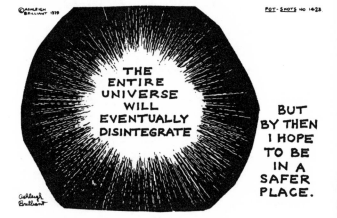

©ASHLEIGH BRILLIANT 1979

THE
ENTIRE
UNIVERSE
WILL
EVENTUALLY
DISINTEGRATE

BUT
BY THEN
I HOPE
TO BE
IN A
SAFER
PLACE.

I HOPE THERE IS A NEXT WORLD,

Ashleigh Brilliant

BECAUSE I'LL DEFINITELY NEED ANOTHER LIFE TO UNDERSTAND THIS ONE.

POT-SHOTS No. 1672. © 1980 Ashleigh Brilliant.

POT SHOTS No. 1365. © Brilliant Enterprises 1977.

If God knew
I would lose anyway,
Why did he make me
Try so hard to win?

Ashleigh Brilliant

©BRILLIANT ENTERPRISES 1974

I DON'T KNOW HOW TO BE HAPPY—

They didn't teach it in my school.

Ashleigh Brilliant

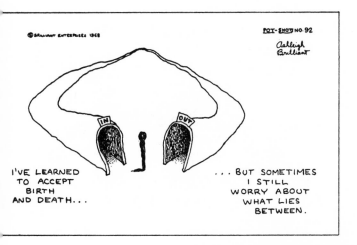

©BRILLIANT ENTERPRISES 1968 POT-SHOTS NO. 92

Ashleigh Brilliant

IN

OUT

I'VE LEARNED TO ACCEPT BIRTH AND DEATH...

...BUT SOMETIMES I STILL WORRY ABOUT WHAT LIES BETWEEN.

Ashleigh Brilliant

IT'S ALL VERY SIMPLE,
OR ELSE IT'S ALL VERY COMPLEX,

OR PERHAPS IT'S NEITHER, OR BOTH.

POT SHOTS No 1685 ©1980 Ashleigh Brilliant

IT'S TECHNOLOGICALLY POSSIBLE TO CREATE HEAVEN ON EARTH,

BUT THE COST WOULD BE ASTRONOMICAL.

© BRILLIANT ENTERPRISES 1976

SOMEDAY THERE'LL BE BOOKS EXPLAINING WHAT'S HAPPENING NOW,

BUT BY THEN, I MAY HAVE LOST INTEREST.

© BRILLIANT ENTERPRISES 1977.

© ASHLEIGH BRILLIANT 1973

ONE THING YOU CAN RELY ON

IS THAT THERE WILL ALWAYS BE UNCERTAINTY.

IN ORDER TO GET
FROM WHAT WAS
TO WHAT WILL BE,
YOU MUST
GO THROUGH
WHAT IS.

© Brilliant Enterprises 1975.

Don't be
afraid
to give
some of
yourself
away...

It will all
grow back.

POT SHOTS No. 892 © Brilliant Enterprises 1976.

Life is not a problem ~

Life is the closest
God has yet come
to a solution.

POT-SHOTS No. 1701. © 1980 Ashleigh Brilliant.

Pot-Shots ✳ BY ASHLEIGH BRILLIANT

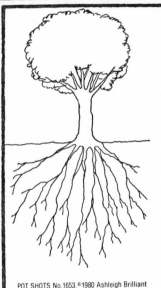

I can't
trace my family
back very far,
but still
proudly believe
that I too
had ancestors.

POT SHOTS No.1653.©1980 Ashleigh Brilliant

Ashleigh
Brilliant

The Family, and Other Strange Groups

Human relationships take many odd forms, the family being perhaps one of the oddest. By sheer biological accident, we are thrown together with a group of strangers with whom, in many cases, we would otherwise never have chosen to associate.

Families cannot be rented, bought, or stolen. They can be found, and occasionally lost, but sometimes, if you try to lose one, it will follow you. Families usually begin with, and are often enlarged by, a form of conquest known as "marriage." But most new family members arrive by means of an elaborate delivery system called "birth." They come unwillingly, like refugees, hungry, tired, penniless, utterly without possessions, and totally ignorant of the country they are entering. Traditionally, small volunteer teams of sponsors known as "parents" supply them with basic necessities and help them learn to cope with the strange local language and customs.

Like politicians, however, parents, although given great powers over human lives, are not required to pass any special examinations to prove themselves qualified for their tasks. The result, in many instances, can be somebody like you or like me.

I PREFER GROUP ACTIVITY BECAUSE, EVEN IF IT'S FOOLISH, AT LEAST I'M NOT THE ONLY FOOL.

©ASHLEIGH BRILLIANT 1969.

POT-SHOTS NO. 1279.

SOMETHING MUST BE WRONG IF I GET HOMESICK EVEN WHEN I'M AT HOME.

© BRILLIANT ENTERPRISES 1977.

Ashleigh Brilliant

© ASHLEIGH BRILLIANT 1979.

PARENTS AND THEIR CHILDREN ARE NOT NATURAL FRIENDS

BUT,
IN CERTAIN CASES,
LIFELONG
ATTACHMENTS
HAVE BEEN
FORMED.

Ashleigh Brilliant

© ASHLEIGH BRILLIANT 1979.

SOMEHOW I FAILED IN THE EDUCATION OF MY PARENTS, BUT I DON'T KNOW WHERE I WENT WRONG.

Ashleigh Brilliant

THE FUTURE IS DESCENDED FROM THE PAST,

AND SO, NATURALLY, OFTEN BEARS A CLOSE FAMILY RESEMBLANCE.

Ashleigh Brilliant ©ASHLEIGH BRILLIANT 1979

Ashleigh Brilliant

IS IT HARDER TO BE THE PARENT OF A CHILD,

OR THE CHILD OF A PARENT?

©BRILLIANT ENTERPRISES 1976.

THE ONLY THING WORSE THAN THE DIFFICULTIES OF GROWING UP

ARE THE DIFFICULTIES OF BEING GROWN UP.

Ashleigh Brilliant

POT SHOTS No.1670.©1980 Ashleigh Brilliant

©ASHLEIGH BRILLIANT 1979.

POT-SHOTS NO. 1562.

IF I CAN'T DO ANYTHING ELSE FOR YOU,

at least I can worry about you.

Ashleigh Brilliant

I ALWAYS CRY AT WEDDINGS,

ESPECIALLY MY OWN.

POT-SHOTS Nº. 725. © 1980 Ashleigh Brilliant.

MISSING —

PRESUMED MARRIED.

POT SHOTS No. 1257. © Brilliant Enterprises 1977.

: POT SHOTS No. 534. © Brilliant Enterprises 1974.

EVEN WHEN YOU'RE MARRIED, LIFE, SOMEHOW, MUST STILL GO ON.

© BRILLIANT ENTERPRISES 1972

Ashleigh
Brilliant

THE ONLY REAL STRAIN ON OUR MARRIAGE

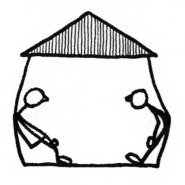

COMES FROM TRYING TO LIVE TOGETHER.

© BRILLIANT ENTERPRISES 1975.

Ashleigh
Brilliant

IT MIGHT HELP US TO STAY TOGETHER

IF WE SPENT MORE TIME APART.

© BRILLIANT ENTERPRISES 1977.

IS THERE ROOM IN THIS MARRIAGE FOR BOTH OF US?

Ashleigh Brilliant

HOW CAN I GET OUT OF THIS MARRIAGE,

Ashleigh Brilliant

WITHOUT DESTROYING IT?

© ASHLEIGH BRILLIANT 1979

114

POT-SHOTS NO. 935.

© BRILLIANT ENTERPRISES 1976

LET'S DEFY COMMON SENSE,

AND TRY TO BE

HAPPY TOGETHER.

Ashleigh
Brilliant

115

© BRILLIANT ENTERPRISES 1977.

POT-SHOTS NO. 1318.

MY LIFE
IS A
PERFORMANCE

FOR WHICH
I WAS NEVER
GIVEN

ANY CHANCE
TO REHEARSE.

The Way It Is (Apparently)

Trying to write or think about life while actually wandering somewhere in it must be something like attemping to make a study of water while totally submerged. Yet the thought-bubbles persistently form, and somehow my little messages squeeze into them, to stage miniature wrestling-matches with reality. The reader too is, I realize, somewhat handicapped by being alive. And an increasing number of my readers have actually incurred this handicap since I first began publishing these thoughts. But we must all try to make the best of this situation. And it does at least enhance the daily show in which we play both participants and audience with a certain "you are there" quality.

Of course, I know no more about life than you do, and possibly much less. All I have, by some fluke, is the ability to take small pieces of it and wrap words around them. I make no special claim for these little parcels, except that they are guaranteed to cure any ailment caused by a lack of POT-SHOTS.

117

©BRILLIANT ENTERPRISES 1974

IT WOULD BE EASIER
TO PLAY MY PART IN LIFE

IF I HAD
   A COPY OF
      THE SCRIPT.

Ashleigh
Brilliant

POT-SHOTS NO. 1103.

ALL I ASK
   IS THAT
THE PRESENT MOMENT
   BE POSTPONED
      UNTIL I'M
      READY FOR IT.

©BRILLIANT ENTERPRISES 1977. Ashleigh Brilliant

INCREDIBLE
AS IT SEEMS,

MY LIFE
IS BASED ON
A TRUE STORY.

Ashleigh Brilliant

©BRILLIANT ENTERPRISES 1975.

THERE ARE SO MANY THINGS
I CAN'T DO,
JUST BECAUSE
I'M
HUMAN.

Ashleigh
Brilliant

POT SHOTS No. 1746 ©1980 Ashleigh Brilliant

MY MAIN
OBJECT IN
LIFE IS TO
SEE WHAT
WILL HAPPEN
NEXT.

POT SHOTS No. 1703 ©1980 Ashleigh Brilliant

LOOK HOW OFTEN THE UNEXPECTED HAPPENS~

AND YET WE STILL NEVER EXPECT IT!

POT SHOTS No.1662.©1980 Ashleigh Brilliant

Ashleigh Brilliant

©BRILLIANT ENTERPRISES 1975.

POT-SHOTS NO.872.

SOMETIMES IT SEEMS LIFE IS JUST A LONG SERIES OF INTERRUPTIONS

Ashleigh Brilliant

IF YOU NEVER TRY ANYTHING NEW, YOU'LL MISS MANY OF THE WORLD'S GREAT DISAPPOINTMENTS.

POT SHOTS No. 1669 ©1980 Ashleigh Brilliant

© BRILLIANT ENTERPRISES 1977.   POT-SHOTS NO. 1315.

I'VE NEVER LIVED THIS LIFE BEFORE...

PLEASE DON'T TELL ME HOW IT ENDS.

© BRILLIANT ENTERPRISES 1969   POT-SHOTS NO. 125

TAKE COURAGE!

WHATEVER YOU DECIDE TO DO, IT WILL PROBABLY BE THE WRONG THING.

UNLESS YOU MOVE,

THE PLACE
WHERE YOU ARE
IS THE PLACE
WHERE YOU
WILL
ALWAYS BE.

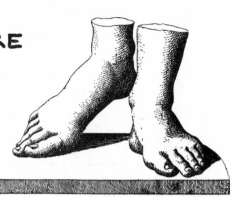

POT SHOTS No.1726.©1980 Ashleigh Brilliant

Ashleigh Brilliant

© BRILLIANT ENTERPRISES 1969

MY LIFE HAS A SUPERB CAST,
BUT I CAN'T
FIGURE OUT THE PLOT.

POT-SHOTS NO. 144

Ashleigh
Brilliant

© BRILLIANT ENTERPRISES 1976

POT-SHOTS NO. 954.

CAN THIS REALLY BE MY LIFE?

OR HAS THERE BEEN SOME MISTAKE?

Ashleigh Brilliant

POT-SHOTS NO. 1273.

IT'S EASIER TO SEE HOW FUNNY LIFE IS

WHEN SOMEBODY ELSE IS LIVING IT.

Ashleigh Brilliant

© BRILLIANT ENTERPRISES 1977.

Ashleigh Brilliant

HAPPINESS
IS TOO EASY
TO LOSE ~

NEXT TIME
I FIND SOME,
I'M GOING TO
HIDE IT.

POT SHOTS No.1681.©1980 Ashleigh Brilliant

124

WHERE DID YOU PUT THAT GOOD TIME I WAS PLANNING TO HAVE?

Ashleigh Brilliant

POT SHOTS No.1733.©1980 Ashleigh Brilliant

© BRILLIANT ENTERPRISES 1972

POT-SHOTS NO. 372

IF ONLY I WERE HAVING AS MUCH FUN AS YOU PROBABLY THINK I AM.

Ashleigh Brilliant

WHEN LIFE BECOMES TOO PAINFUL, I TRY TO THINK ABOUT SOMETHING ELSE.

Ashleigh Brilliant

POT SHOTS No.1720.©1980 Ashleigh Brilliant

126

WHY IS THERE
SO OFTEN
SO LITTLE
RESEMBLANCE

Ashleigh Brilliant

BETWEEN
WHAT I WANTED
AND
WHAT I GET?

© BRILLIANT ENTERPRISES 1977.

MEETING PEOPLE
WHO'VE HAD SOME OF
THE GREAT EXPERIENCES
I'VE MISSED

Ashleigh Brilliant

SOMETIMES
MAKES ME FEEL
VERY LUCKY.

© ASHLEIGH BRILLIANT 1978.

© ASHLEIGH BRILLIANT 1979.

I TRY TO TAKE ONE DAY AT A TIME,

BUT SOMETIMES SEVERAL DAYS ATTACK ME AT ONCE.

Ashleigh Brilliant

Ashleigh Brilliant

I CAN FACE ANYTHING,

EXCEPT THE FUTURE,

AND CERTAIN PARTS OF THE PAST AND PRESENT.

POT SHOTS No.1698.©1980 Ashleigh Brilliant

RIGHT NOW
I'M WORKING ON
A FASCINATING PROJECT:

STAYING ALIVE.

© BRILLIANT ENTERPRISES 1969

**IF
THIS IS ALL
LIFE CAN BE,**

Ashleigh
Brilliant

I'M SORRY
IT'S NOT BETTER,
BUT GLAD
IT'S NOT WORSE.

POT SHOTS No. 1656. © 1980 Ashleigh Brilliant

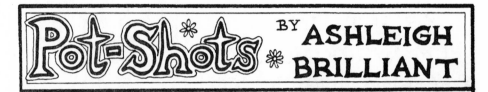

To get to
a good place,
sometimes
you have to
go through
a number of
bad places.

POT SHOTS No.1659. © 1980 Ashleigh Brilliant

Ashleigh Brilliant

Travel, and Other Wild Pursuits

Confined to the Earth and its environs, we entertain ourselves by changing location physically and mentally. Travel is popular because (as some genius has written in my previous book) it makes you feel you are getting somewhere. My own travels, however, have usually ended with coming home again. Perhaps that is an almost inevitable result of living on a round planet.

Fortunately, mine is the kind of work which can be done quite easily while traveling, and is often stimulated by it, sometimes in unexpected ways. Once, for example, in 1969, Dorothy and I found ourselves on a Brazilian river-boat sailing down the Amazon. She enjoyed sitting by the rail for hours at a time, watching the jungle go by. I eventually became bored with this, and, retreating on one occasion to our cabin, uttered and recorded the words destined to become POT-SHOT No. 126: "LET ME KNOW EVERYTHING THAT'S BEEN GOING ON — I'D HATE TO MISS ANY OF THE MONOTONY."

©BRILLIANT ENTERPRISES 1975   POT- SHOTS NO. 401

ALL THIS RELAXATION

HAS EXHAUSTED ME.

POT- SHOTS NO 540

I ADJUST VERY EASILY—

GIVE ME EVERYTHING
I HAD AT HOME,

AND I CAN LIVE
ANYWHERE.

132

SHALL WE SAIL ON THE TITANIC,

OR WAIT TO FLY ON THE HINDENBURG?

Ashleigh Brilliant

© BRILLIANT ENTERPRISES 1977.

© BRILLIANT ENTERPRISES 1971

IT'S EASY TO COME AND GO...

Ashleigh Brilliant

THE HARD THING IS TO REMAIN.

© BRILLIANT ENTERPRISES 1969

PROMISE ME YOU WON'T ACCOMPLISH ANYTHING WHILE I'M AWAY.

© BRILLIANT ENTERPRISES 1969

LET ME KNOW EVERYTHING THAT'S BEEN GOING ON — I'D HATE TO MISS ANY OF THE MONOTONY.

134

© BRILLIANT ENTERPRISES 1971

BY THE TIME
YOU KNOW WHERE I AM,
I MAY VERY WELL
BE SOMEWHERE ELSE.

Ashleigh
Brilliant

THE ONLY
KNOWN WAY
TO COVER
MORE DISTANCE
IN LESS TIME

POT SHOTS No 1524

IS
TO GO
FASTER.

Ashleigh
Brilliant

© ASHLEIGH BRILLIANT 1978

FOR SOME
STRANGE REASON,

NO MATTER
WHERE I GO,

THE PLACE
IS ALWAYS CALLED
"HERE."

Ashleigh
Brilliant

POT SHOTS No.1649. ©1980 Ashleigh Brilliant

135

POT-SHOTS NO. 687.

© BRILLIANT ENTERPRISES 1974.

What good is a superior mind, without another superior mind to communicate with?

Go Away Closer

The world is full of friends, lovers, and strangers, many of them very carelessly labelled, so that we are never sure which is which. Even a best friend or dearest lover can turn out, sometimes after many years, to be a cleverly disguised stranger. Hence, a certain caution is necessary in many of our relationships — a certain ambiguity which renders most of our contacts more human and less divine.

But love and trust do apparently exist. I, for one, have never publicly denied their existence. On the contrary, some of my messages will be seen to have a very positive tone. I am sometimes accused of being too cynical, but I prefer to think of myself as a realist. Life is not all bad. In fact, life is not all anything, except that it is all life.

POT- SHOTS NO. 890.

WHY
HAS IT TAKEN ME
SO LONG TO TELL YOU

THAT
I FIND IT HARD
TO COMMUNICATE?

©BRILLIANT ENTERPRISES 1976.

©BRILLIANT ENTERPRISES 1968   POT- SHOTS NO. 64

I'M WRITING
TO TELL YOU
I HAVE NOTHING TO SAY

MAY I
HAVE
THE NEXT
HUG?

POT SHOTS No.1690.©1980 Ashleigh Brilliant

138

© ASHLEIGH BRILLIANT 1979.

WORDS ARE A WONDERFUL FORM OF COMMUNICATION,

BUT THEY WILL NEVER REPLACE KISSES AND PUNCHES.

Ashleigh Brilliant

MY SOURCES ARE UNRELIABLE,

Ashleigh Brilliant

BUT THEIR INFORMATION IS FASCINATING.

© BRILLIANT ENTERPRISES 1977.

Why is it so pleasant
seeing without being seen,

and so sad
loving
without
being loved?

Ashleigh Brilliant ©BRILLIANT ENTERPRISES 1977.

Ashleigh
Brilliant

IS IT
MY TURN
YET
TO HAVE
YOUR
ATTENTION?

POT SHOTS No.1744.©1980 Ashleigh Brilliant

HAVE WE
BEEN LOOKING
FOR
EACH OTHER
IN
THE WRONG
PLACES?

POT SHOTS No.1680. ©1980 Ashleigh Brilliant

IF YOU SAY NOTHING
WHEN YOU HAVE
SOMETHING
TO SAY,

YOU ARE
REALLY
TELLING A LIE.

POT SHOTS No.1735.©1980 Ashleigh Brilliant

©BRILLIANT ENTERPRISES 1970.

POT-SHOTS NO.28

IF YOU
BELIEVE
IN ME,
I EXIST.

Ashleigh Brilliant

141

POT-SHOTS NO. 1464.

YOU CAN'T
JUST SUDDENLY
BE MY
FRIEND

Ashleigh
Brilliant

YOU HAVE TO
GO THROUGH
A TRAINING PERIOD.

© ASHLEIGH BRILLIANT 1979.

© BRILLIANT ENTERPRISES 1976.   POT-SHOTS NO. 965.

I DON'T KNOW WHETHER

TO RUN AWAY WITH YOU

or from you.

Ashleigh Brilliant

© BRILLIANT ENTERPRISES 1975.   POT-SHOTS NO. 741.

Ashleigh
Brilliant

YOU AND I
CAN'T POSSIBLY
BE IN LOVE:

It must be
two other
people.

You can't love me as a hobby —

you've got to consider it a career.

Ashleigh Brilliant
© BRILLIANT ENTERPRISES 1977.

THE ONLY WAY

TO AVOID BEING WITHOUT ME

Ashleigh Brilliant

IS TO BE WITH ME.

POT SHOTS No.1729.©1980 Ashleigh Brilliant

IF YOU CAN'T SAY EXACTLY HOW MUCH YOU LOVE ME, TRY TO MAKE A ROUGH ESTIMATE.

POT SHOTS No.1678.©1980 Ashleigh Brilliant

Ashleigh Brilliant

©BRILLIANT ENTERPRISES 1974

POT- SHOTS NO. 674.

*I don't know
Where we belong,
But I'm sure
We belong together.*

Ashleigh Brilliant

144

I'D BE LOST WITH OR WITHOUT YOU.

POT SHOTS No 1717 ©1980 Ashleigh Brilliant

POT-SHOTS NO 1212

IT'S NICE TO HAVE FRIENDS IN HIGH PLACES,

OR EVEN IN LOW PLACES.

©BRILLIANT ENTERPRISES 1977

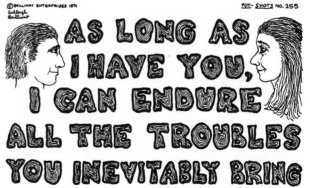

©BRILLIANT ENTERPRISES 1971

POT-SHOTS NO. 255

AS LONG AS I HAVE YOU, I CAN ENDURE ALL THE TROUBLES YOU INEVITABLY BRING

IF ONLY WE DIDN'T HAVE EACH OTHER,

WE COULD STILL LONG FOR EACH OTHER.

POT SHOTS No.1677.©1980 Ashleigh Brilliant

POT-SHOTS NO. 1096.

I will always love

the false image I had of you.

© BRILLIANT ENTERPRISES 1977

© BRILLIANT ENTERPRISES 1972

I'D BE HAPPY TO
COME BACK TO YOU...

Ashleigh
Brilliant

... EXCEPT THAT
IT WAS YOU
WHO WENT AWAY.

© BRILLIANT ENTERPRISES 1977.

Ashleigh
Brilliant

Many things
have changed here,
but my love
is still
exactly where
you left it.

POT-SHOTS NO. 912.

Ashleigh
Brilliant

DUE TO
A SHORTAGE OF
DEVOTED FOLLOWERS,

THE
PRODUCTION OF
GREAT LEADERS
HAS BEEN
DISCONTINUED.

© BRILLIANT ENTERPRISES 1976.

World Affairs,
In An Unfair World

Within the framework of the entire Universe, human life does not seem to be of great significance. Yet, as far as we know, and with all its shortcomings, it is the current champion species. For this reason alone, its affairs would be of some interest. But there is also the fact that we belong to it.

I therefore turn in this last section to the affairs of the wider world, which (as you may have heard) still contains such strange and anachronistic entities as "sovereign" states, mutually unintelligible languages, conflicting currencies, and enormous potentially hostile armed forces. If anybody asked me, I would say that a politically unified, or at least federated, planet is the one thing most worth trying to bring about, and that only then will it become possible to deal effectively with many other human problems. But nobody ever asks me.

Some things
are so forbidden,
they can't even
be mentioned on
lists of
forbidden things.

Ashleigh Brilliant

©BRILLIANT ENTERPRISES 1975.

Ashleigh Brilliant

History records
no more gallant struggle
than that of
humanity
against
the truth.

©BRILLIANT ENTERPRISES 1975.

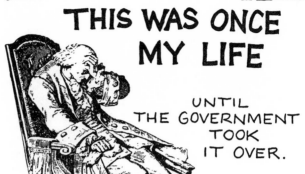

© ASHLEIGH BRILLIANT 1979. POT-SHOTS NO. 1525.

THIS WAS ONCE MY LIFE

UNTIL
THE GOVERNMENT
TOOK
IT OVER.

Ashleigh Brilliant

© BRILLIANT ENTERPRISES 1976 POT-SHOTS NO. 951.

IT'S GOOD TO KNOW THAT,
IF I BEHAVE STRANGELY ENOUGH,

Ashleigh Brilliant

SOCIETY
WILL TAKE
FULL
RESPONSIBILITY
FOR ME.

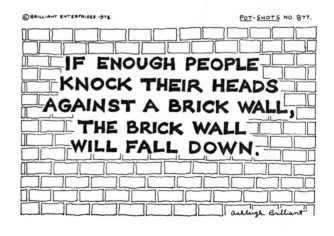

© BRILLIANT ENTERPRISES 1975. POT-SHOTS NO. 877.

IF ENOUGH PEOPLE
KNOCK THEIR HEADS
AGAINST A BRICK WALL,
THE BRICK WALL
WILL FALL DOWN.

Ashleigh Brilliant

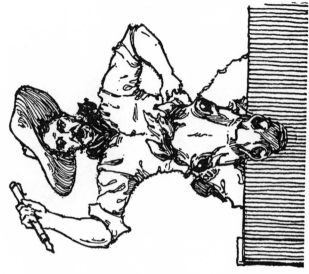

Ashleigh Brilliant

THE PEN IS MIGHTIER THAN THE SWORD ~

SO, IN THIS DANGEROUS WORLD, I ALWAYS CARRY A PEN.

POT SHOTS No.1749.©1980 Ashleigh Brilliant

Ashleigh
Brilliant

CARRY
SOME FREEDOM
WHEREVER
YOU GO—

IT'S
THE ONLY WAY
TO BE SURE OF
A CONSTANT SUPPLY.

©BRILLIANT ENTERPRISES 1977

©BRILLIANT ENTERPRISES 1973

POT-SHOTS NO. 414

I'M SOLIDLY BEHIND
WHICHEVER SIDE
EVENTUALLY
WINS.

Ashleigh
Brilliant

PEOPLE SHOULD NOT
BE TREATED
LIKE CATTLE,

Ashleigh
Brilliant

AND PERHAPS
EVEN CATTLE
SHOULD NOT BE
TREATED LIKE
CATTLE.

SHOTS No 1692 ©1980 Ashleigh Brilliant

HISTORY CLEARLY SHOWS THAT PEOPLE COME, AND PEOPLE GO

BUT, BEYOND THAT, NOTHING ELSE IS VERY CLEAR.

POT SHOTS No 1689 1980 Ashleigh Brilliant

Ashleigh Brilliant

©BRILLIANT ENTERPRISES 1970

POT-SHOTS NO 222

ALL PEOPLE ARE DIFFERENT. THAT'S WHY EVERYBODY SHOULD BE TREATED THE SAME.

POT-SHOTS NO 1418

Ashleigh Brilliant

WHAT GOOD IS FREEDOM, IF IT DOESN'T INCLUDE THE FREEDOM TO TRAMPLE UPON OTHER PEOPLE'S RIGHTS?

© ASHLEIGH BRILLIANT 1979.

I WISH
I KNEW
MORE

ABOUT
THE THINGS
I'M NOT
SUPPOSED TO KNOW
ANYTHING ABOUT.

Ashleigh Brilliant

POT SHOTS No.1667.©1980 Ashleigh Brilliant

THE REALLY GREAT PEOPLE

ARE
THE ONES
WHO
KNOW HOW
TO MAKE
THE
LITTLE PEOPLE
FEEL GREAT.

Ashleigh Brilliant

POT SHOTS No.1682.©1980 Ashleigh Brilliant

Ashleigh
Brilliant

BY STAYING
AT THE
REAR OF THE ADVANCE,

YOU CAN BE
AT THE
FOREFRONT
OF THE RETREAT.

© BRILLIANT ENTERPRISES 1975.

I'M SUPPOSED TO BE
LEADING THE
REVOLUTION—

WHICH WAY
DID IT GO?

Ashleigh
Brilliant

© BRILLIANT ENTERPRISES 1970   POT-SHOTS NO. 200

CERTAIN THINGS ARE WORTH FIGHTING FOR,

IN A CERTAIN WAY, UP TO A CERTAIN POINT.

POT SHOTS No.1730.©1980 Ashleigh Brilliant

I'M LOOKING FOR FREEDOM

— CAN YOU DIRECT ME?

POT SHOTS No.1707.©1980 Ashleigh Brilliant

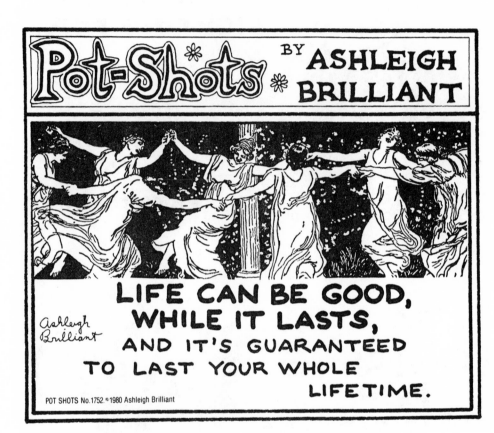

POT SHOTS No.1752. ©1980 Ashleigh Brilliant

The Great Card Game

Through the magic of paper and ink, something of you and something of me has been brought together here. I hope we will go on meeting like this, in all kinds of strange and familiar places. One particularly good place is on my postcards, which provide a very pleasant kind of three-way communication, between me and you and somebody else. I invite you to send for my Catalogue, which lists hundreds of different messages, including many not found in this book. It comes with sample cards and a lovely order form, and also includes information about ordering my books, should you be unable to obtain them locally. The current (1992) price is two U.S. dollars. Please enclose that amount, or its equivalent, in your own time and currency. My address is:

Ashleigh Brilliant
117 W. Valerio St.
Santa Barbara, California 93101, U.S.A.

POT-SHOTS NO. 641

Ashleigh Brilliant

© BRILLIANT ENTERPRISES 1974

LIFE IS A VERY SPECIAL OCCASION!